"Denise's Whimsy Palette: Coloring Serenity "

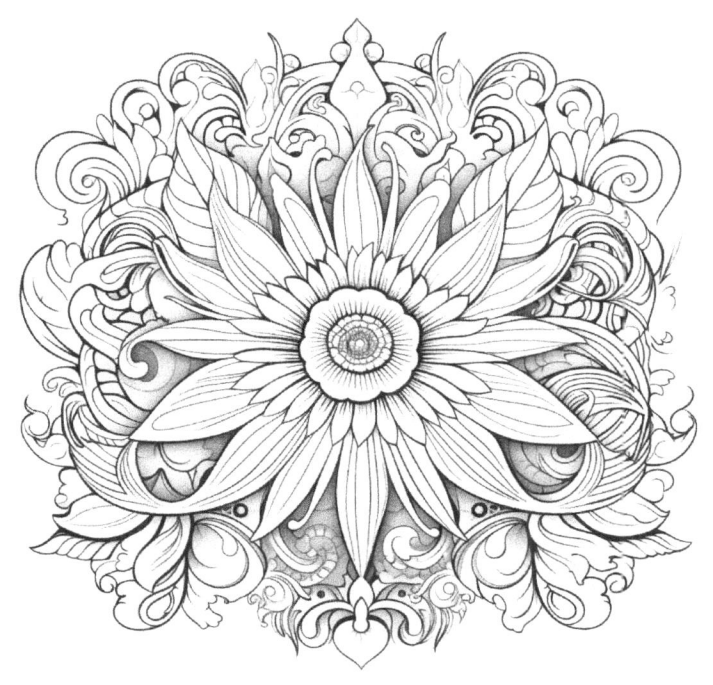

Yogi: ....

"Enter a realm of Serenity through color with Denise's Whimsy Palette "

Dear Readers,

It brings me immense joy to share "Denise's Whimsy Palette: Coloring Serenity" with all of you. This book was crafted with love and the intention of providing you with a momentary escape into a world of artful tranquility. As you color these pages, may you find solace, creativity, and the pure delight that comes from embracing your inner artist. Thank you for being a part of this colorful journey.

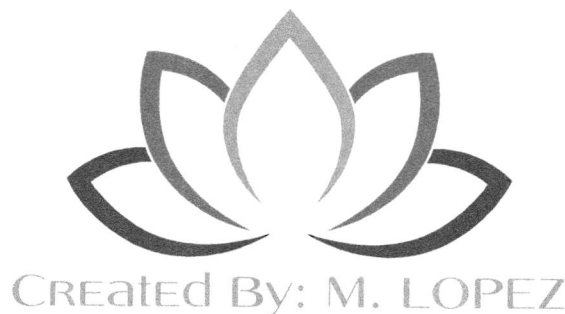

Created By: M. Lopez

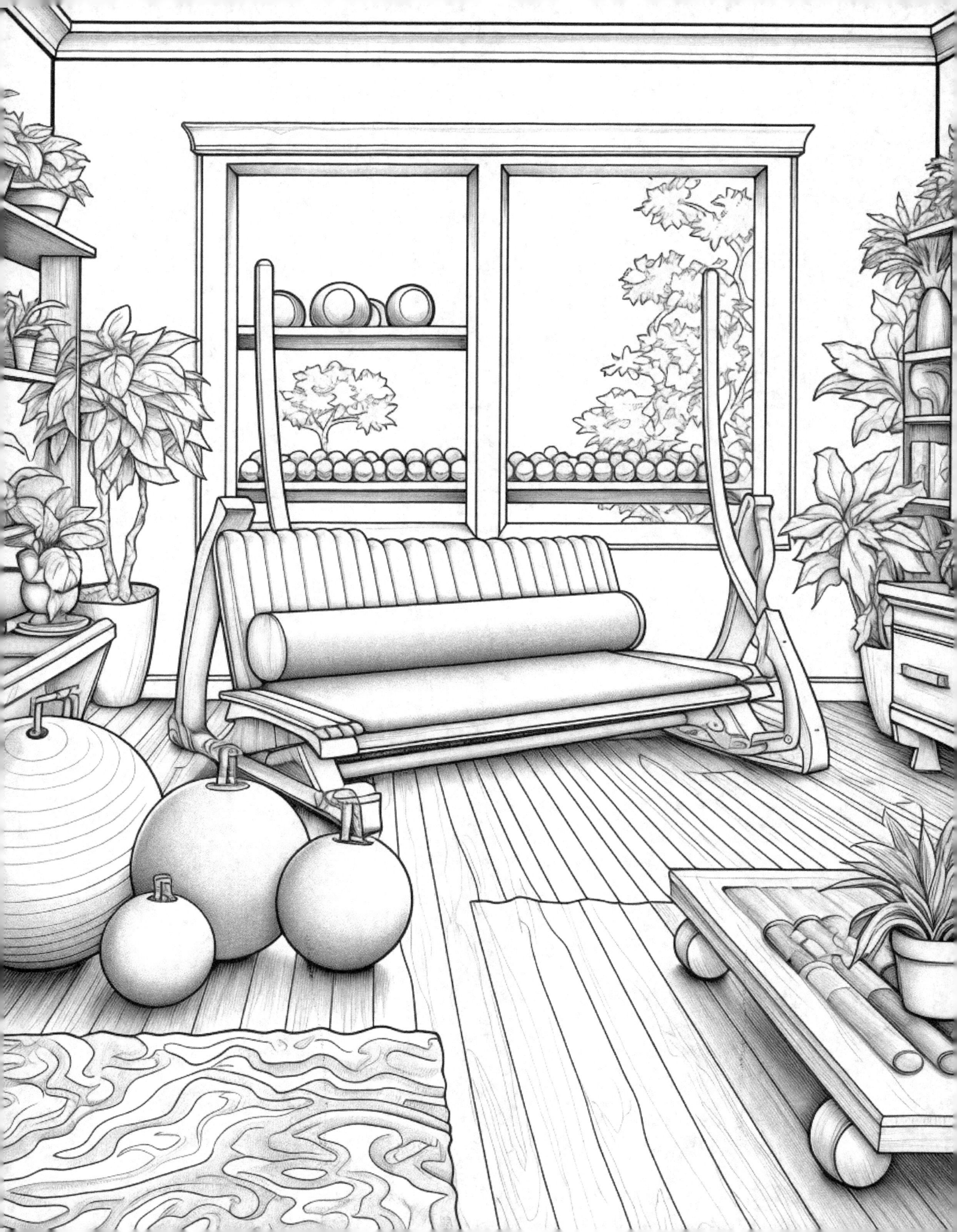

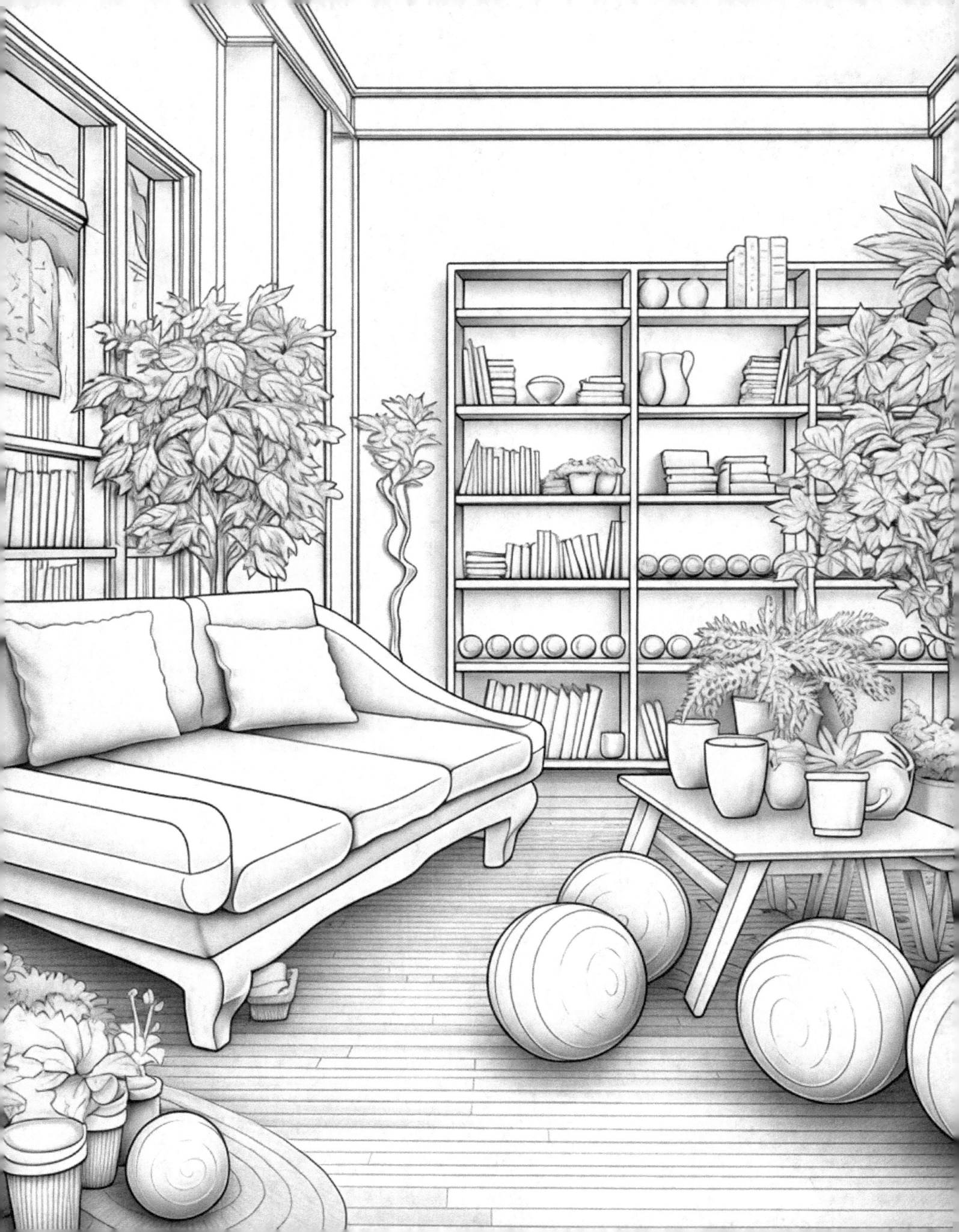

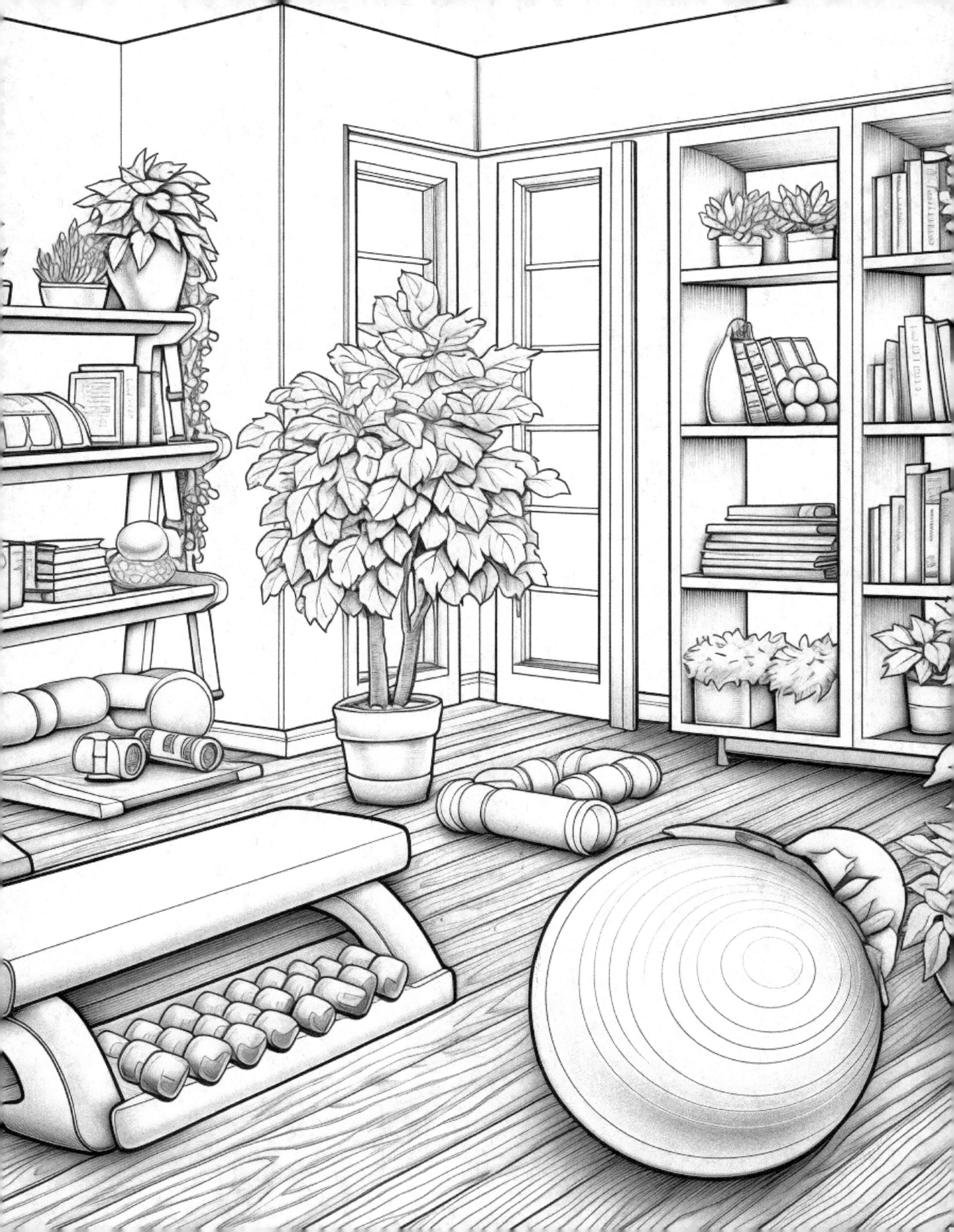

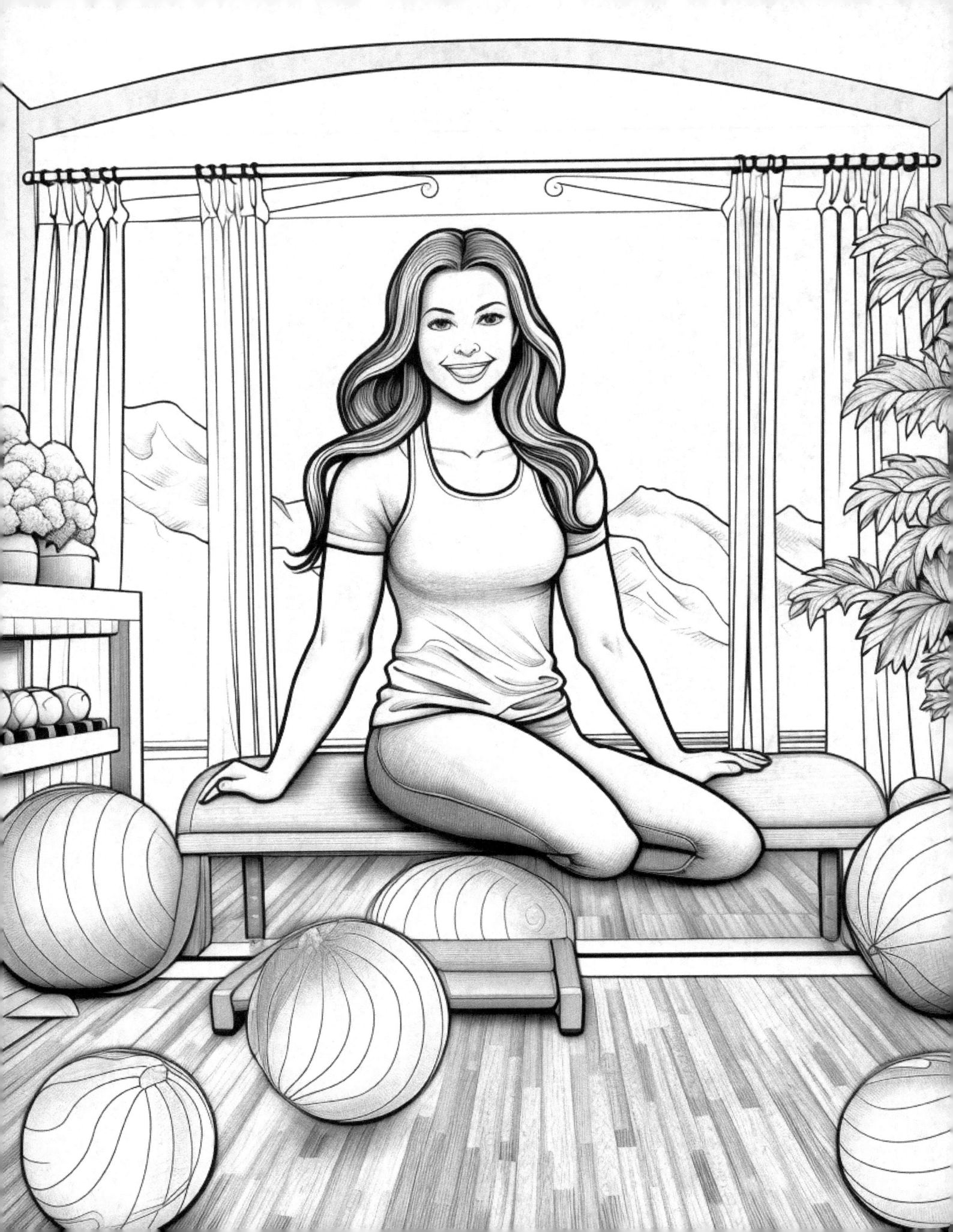

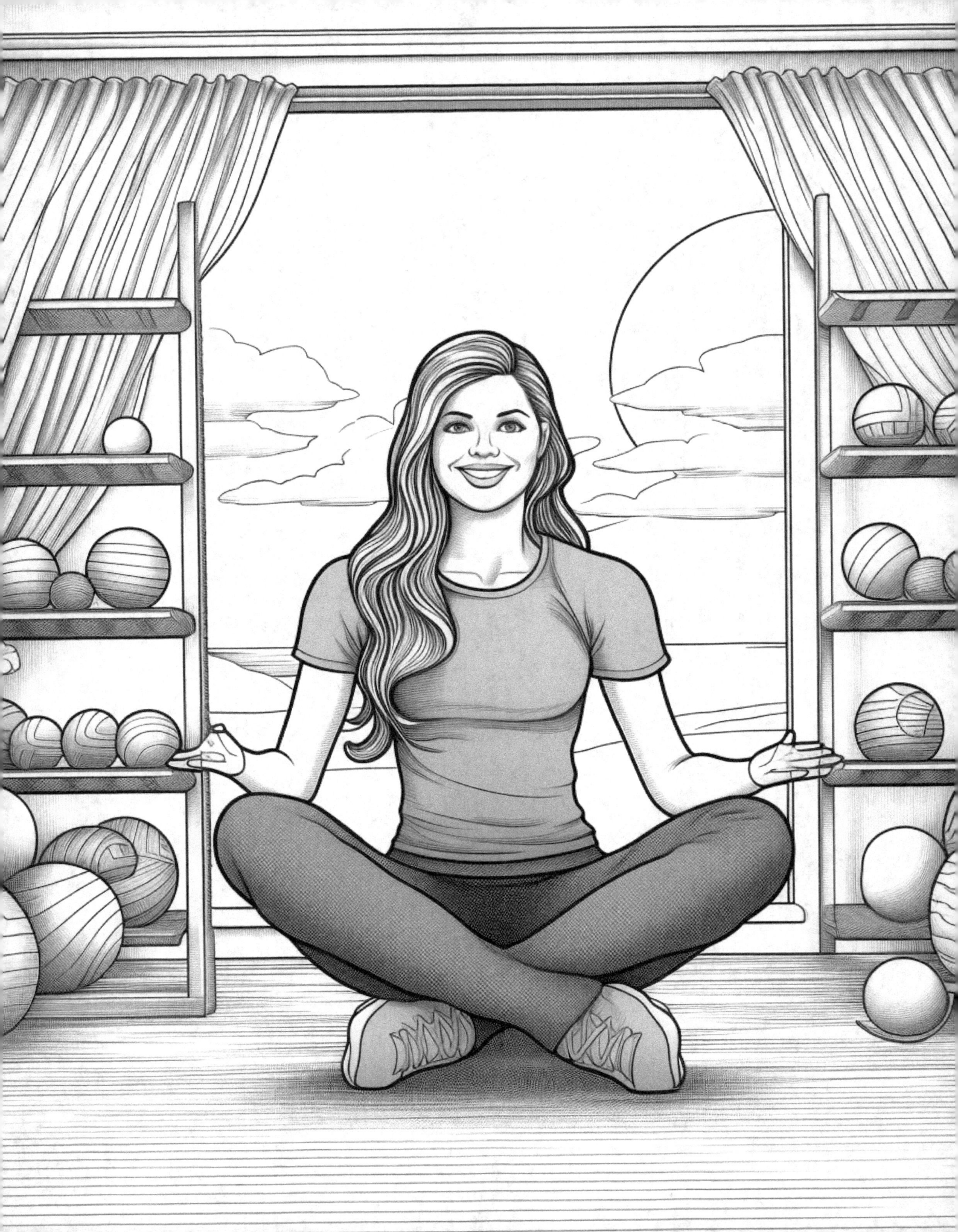

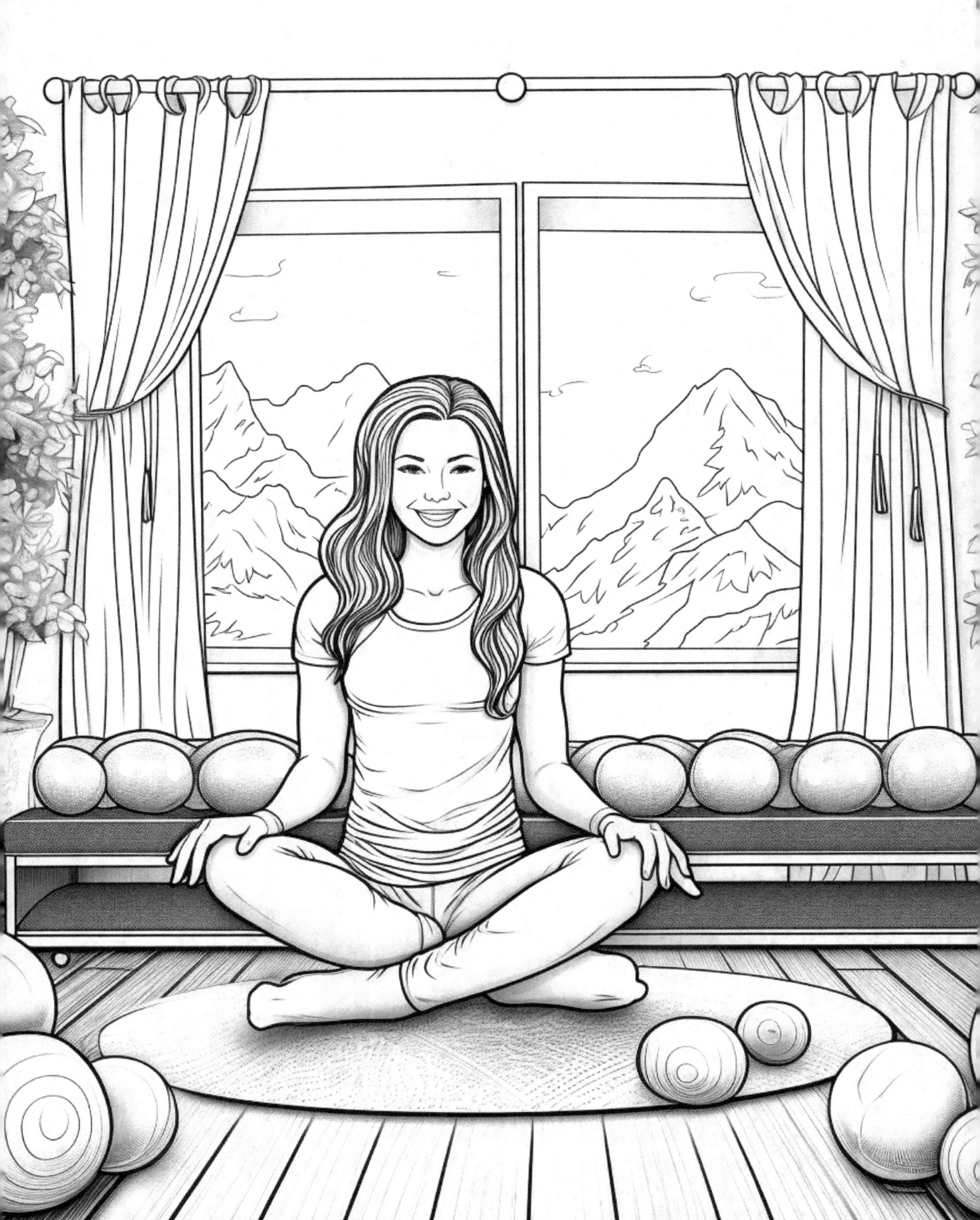

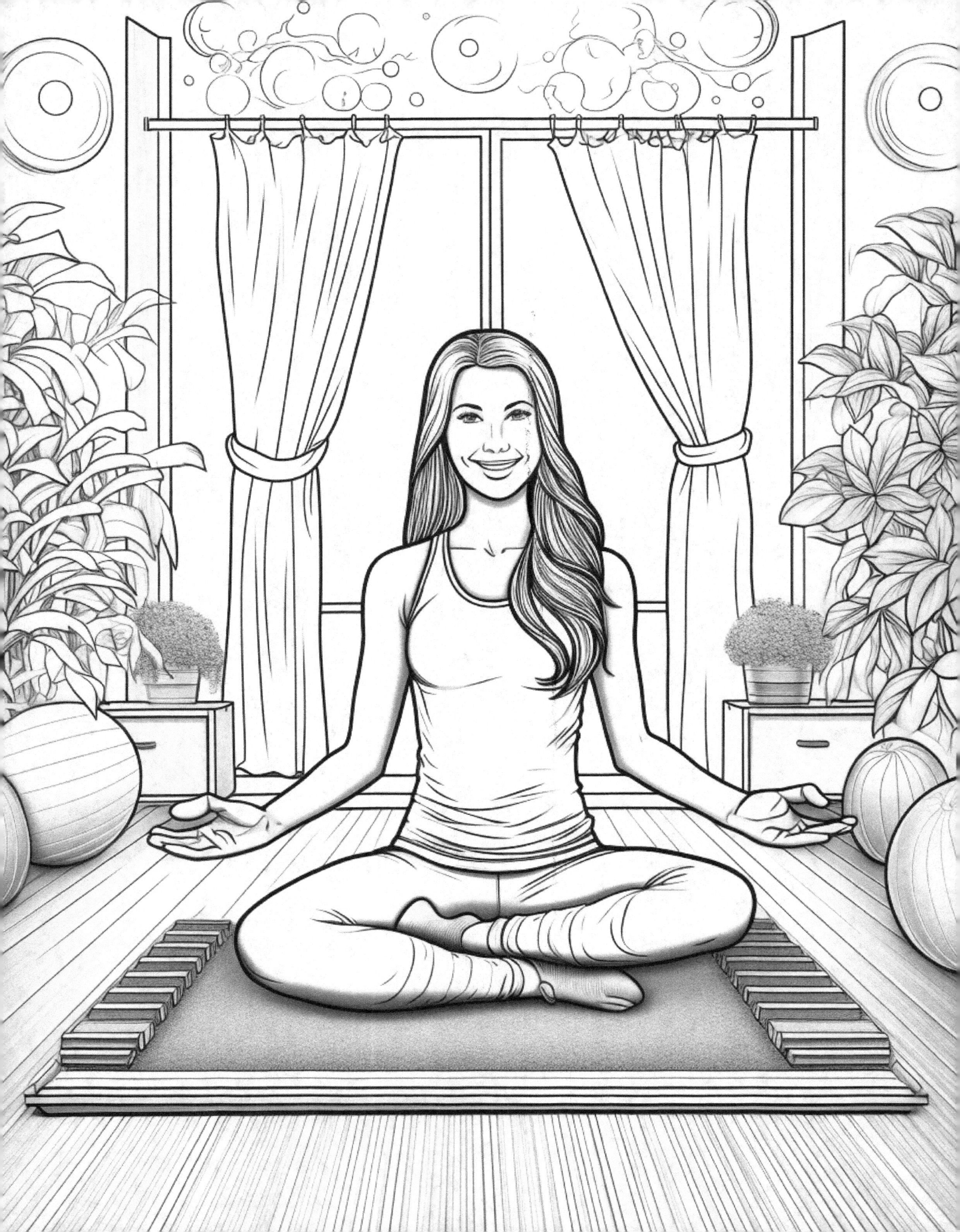

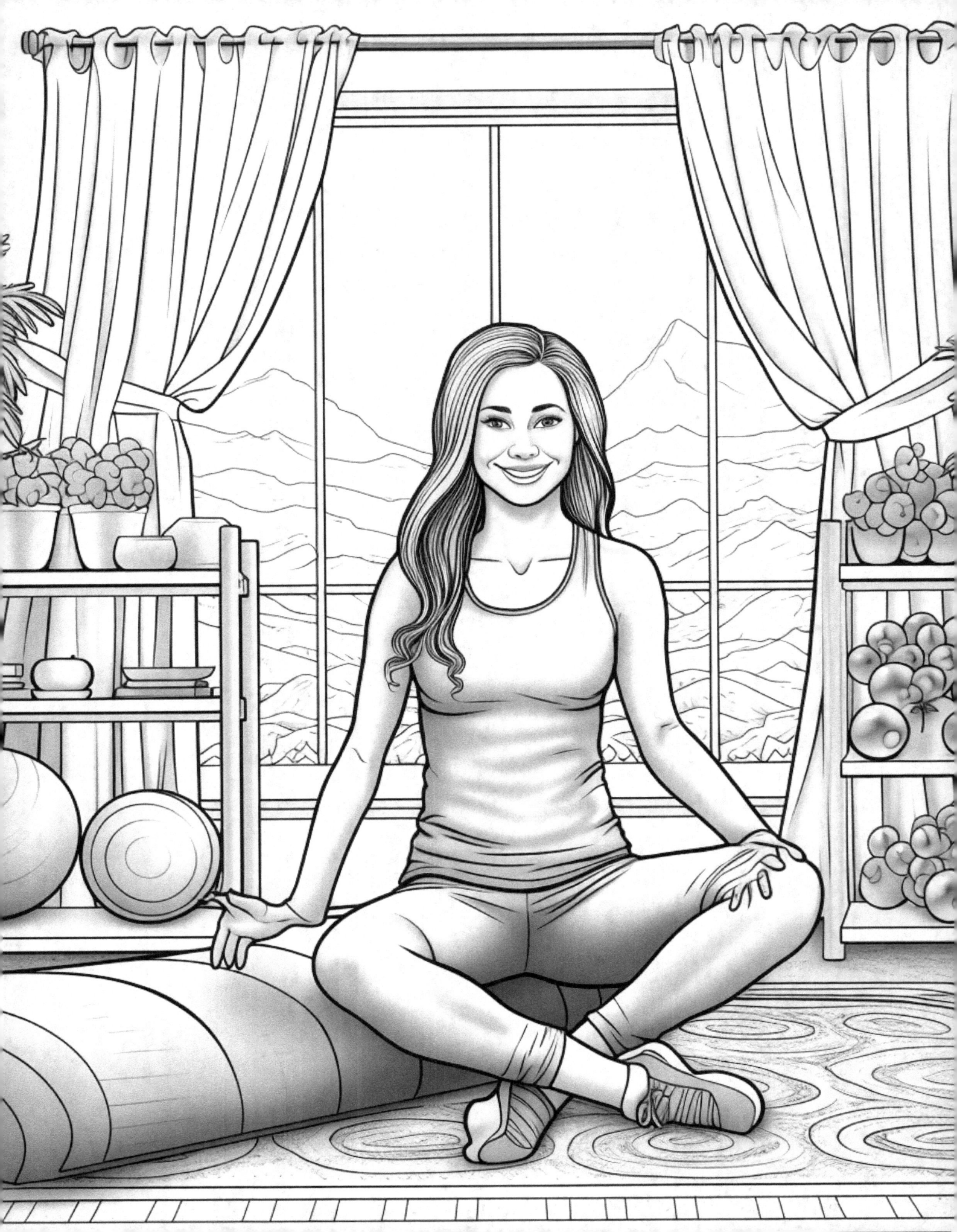

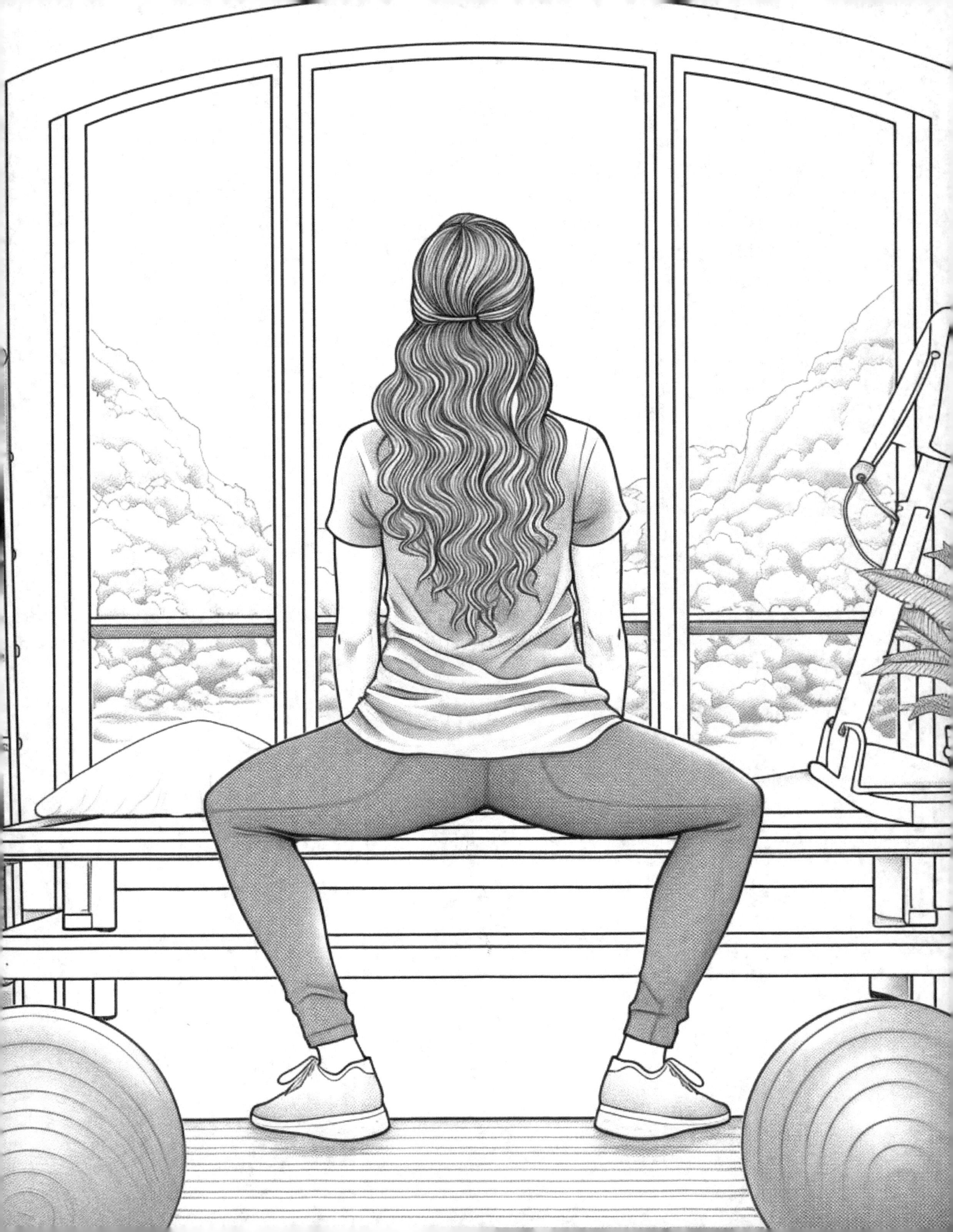

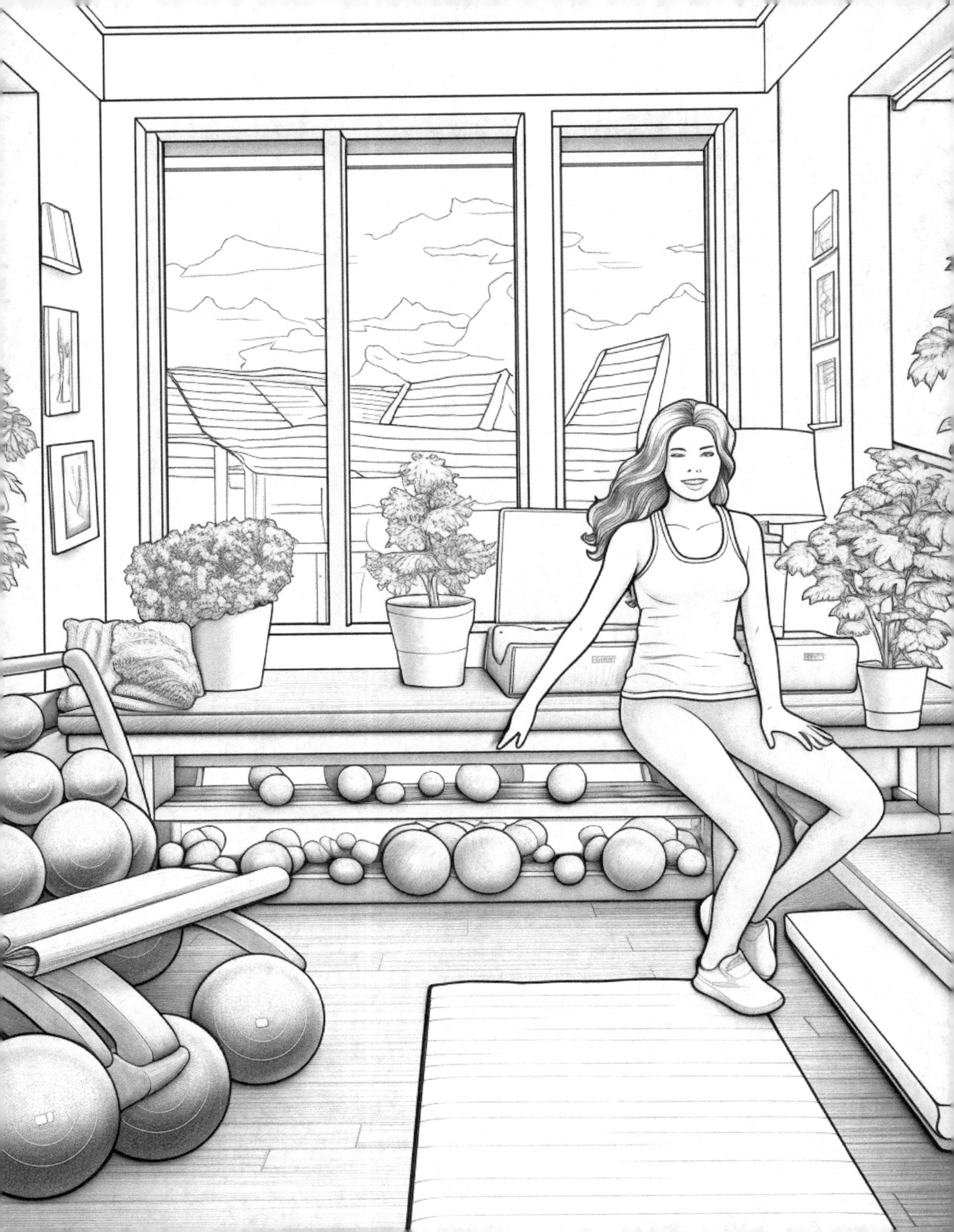

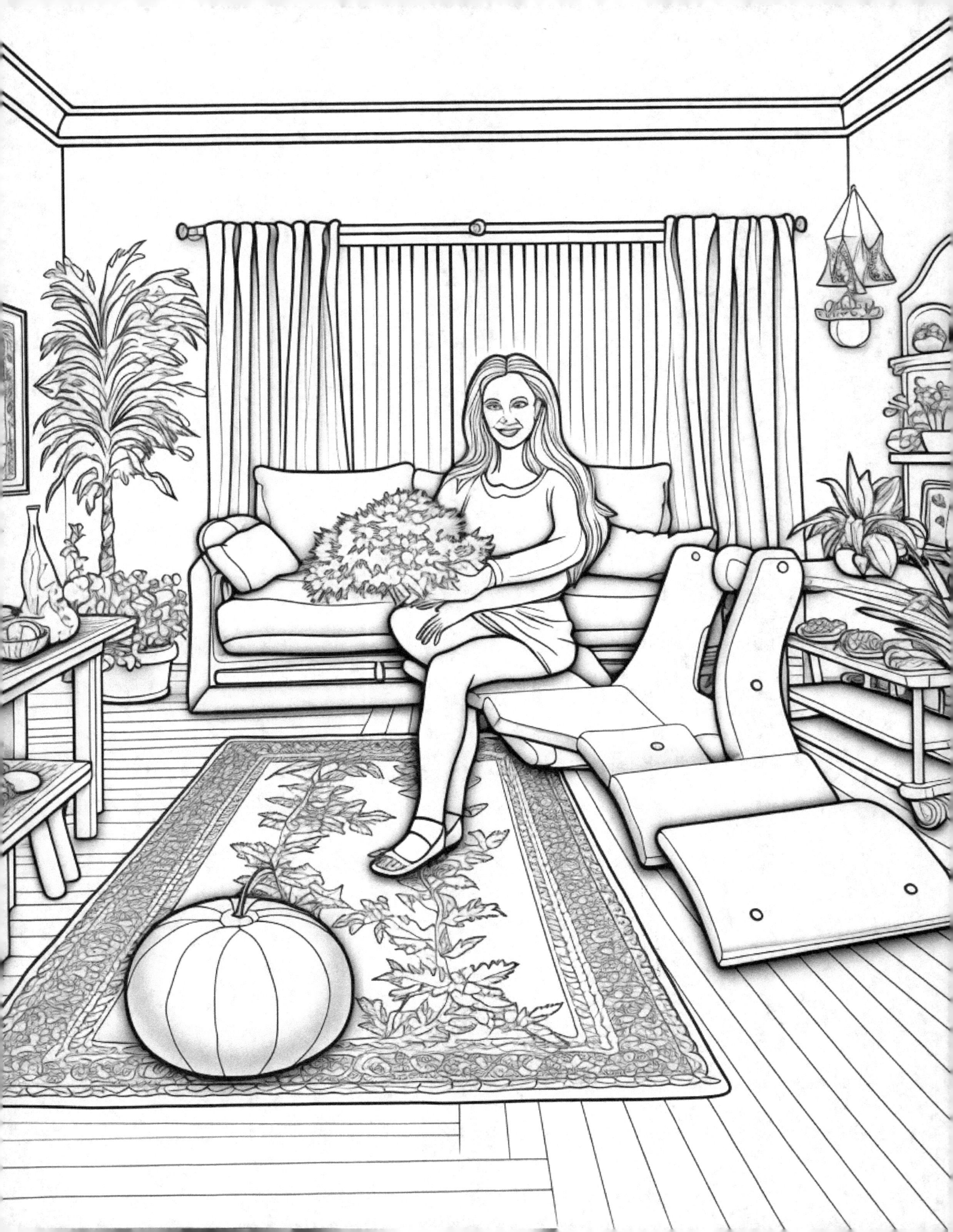

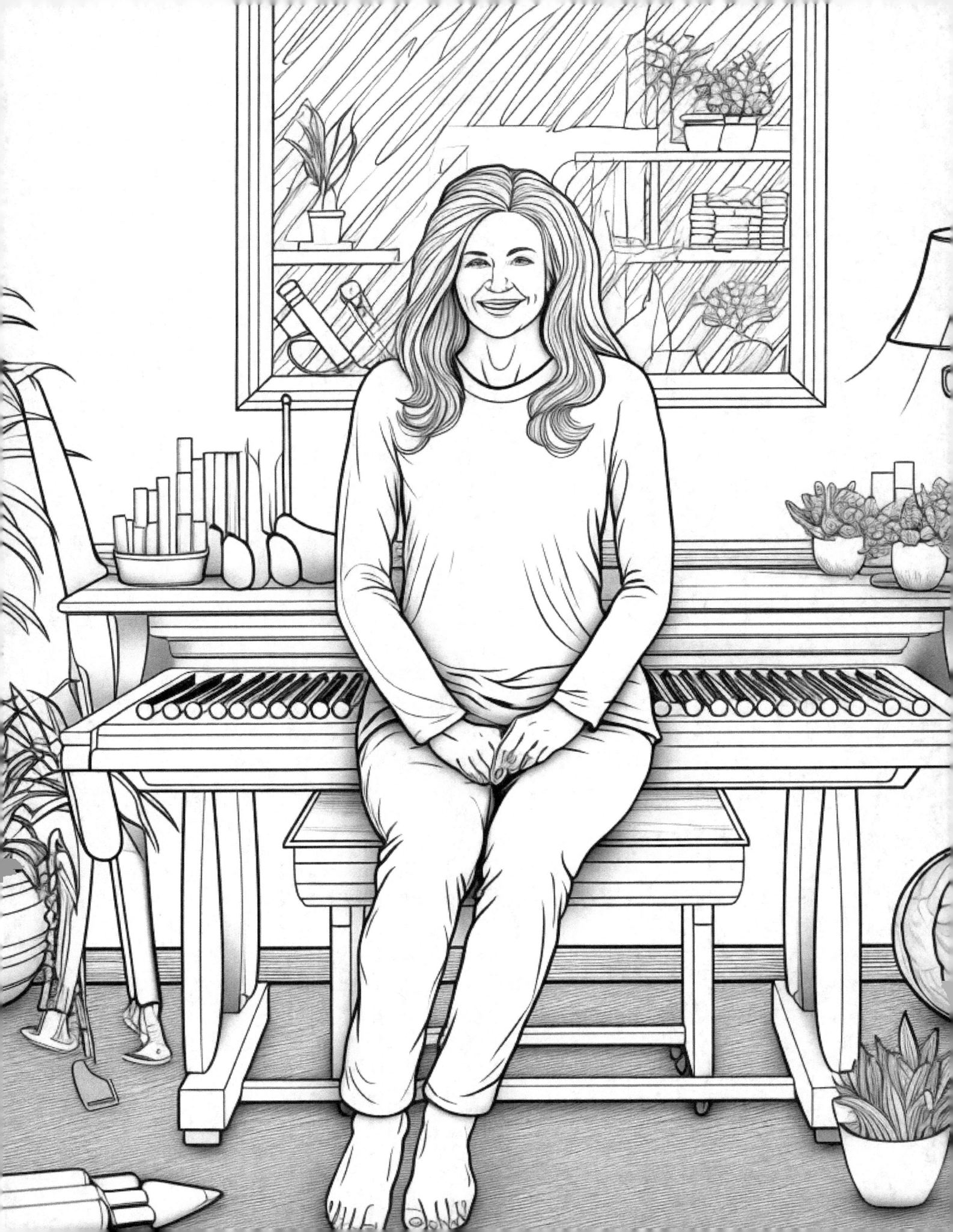

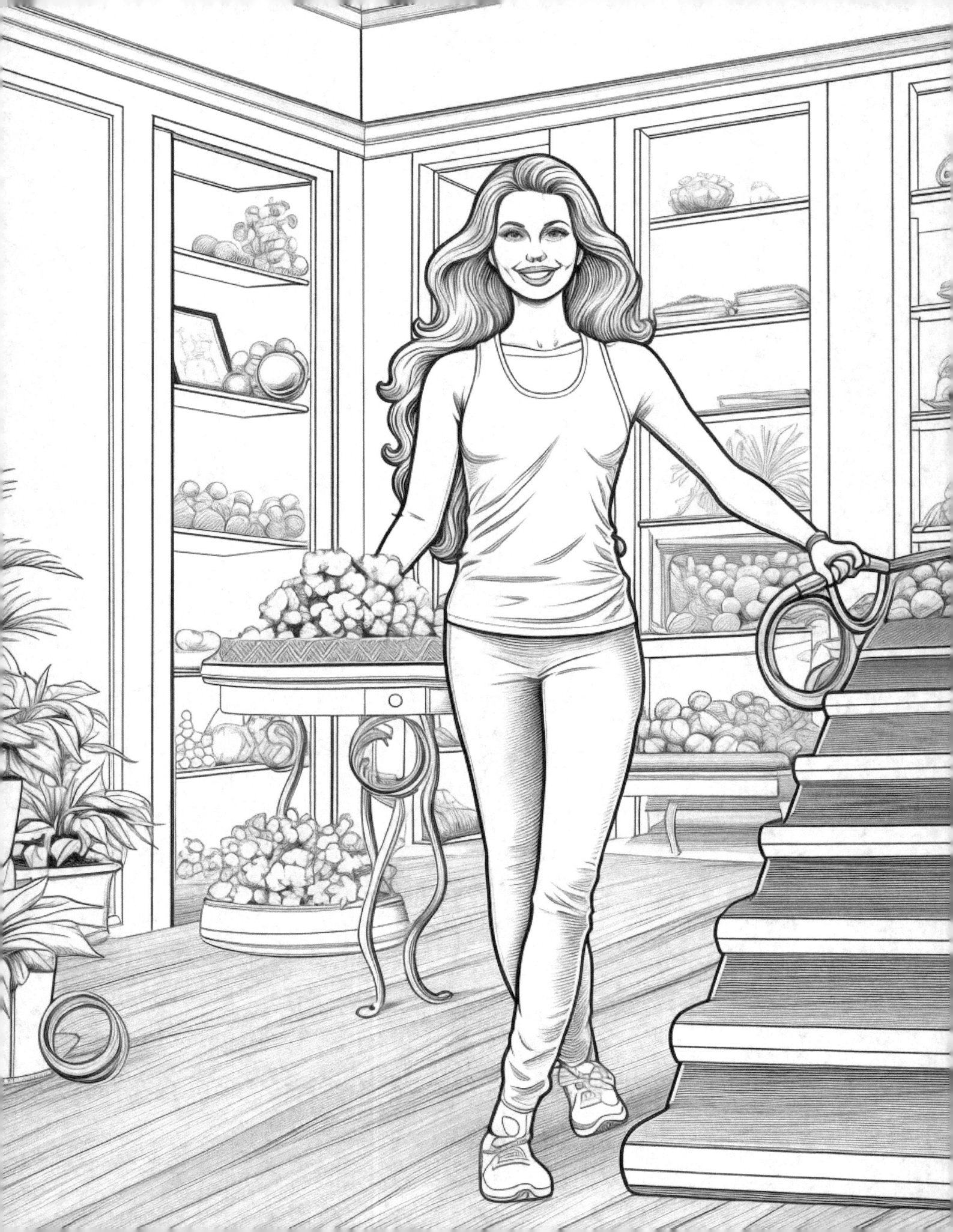

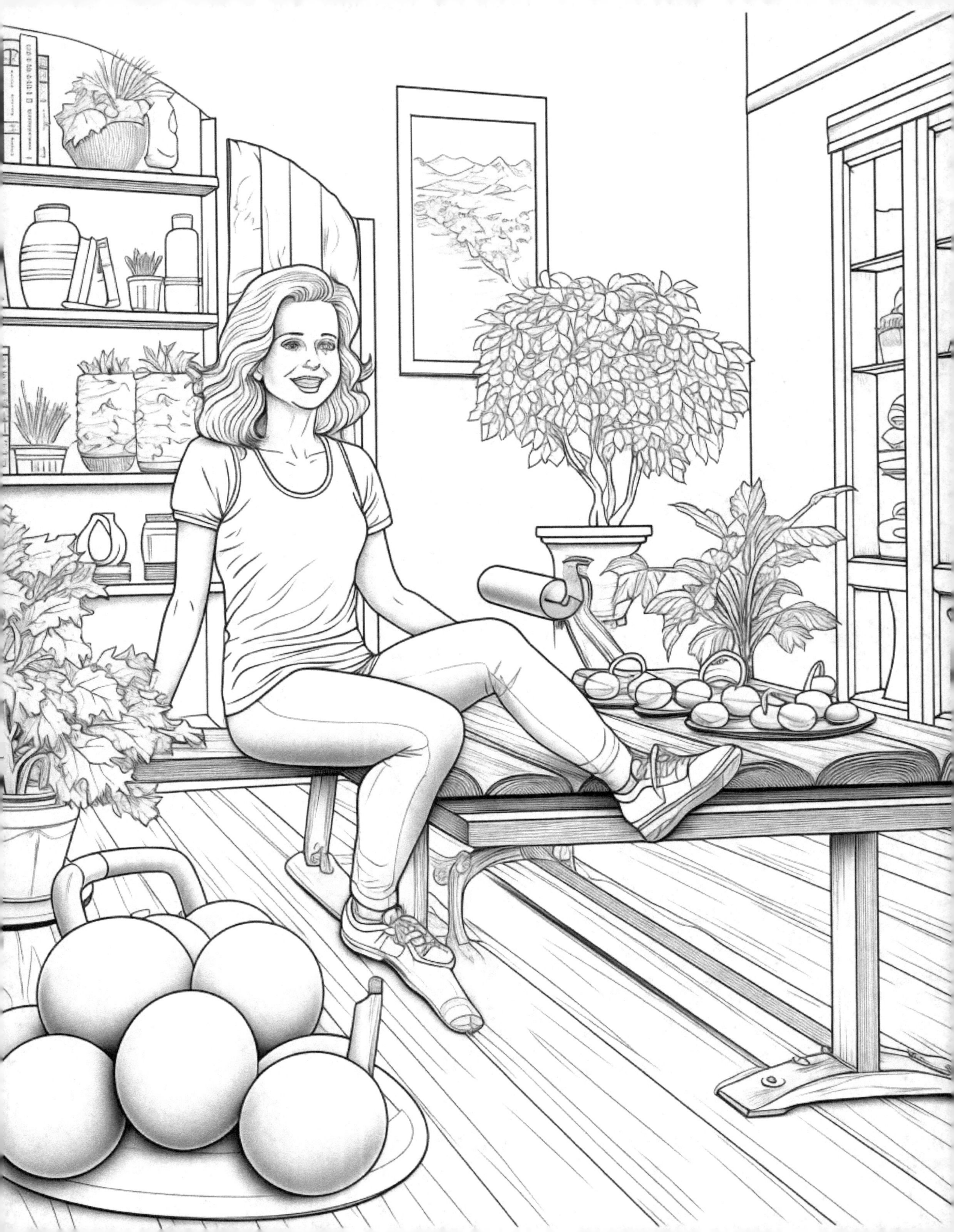

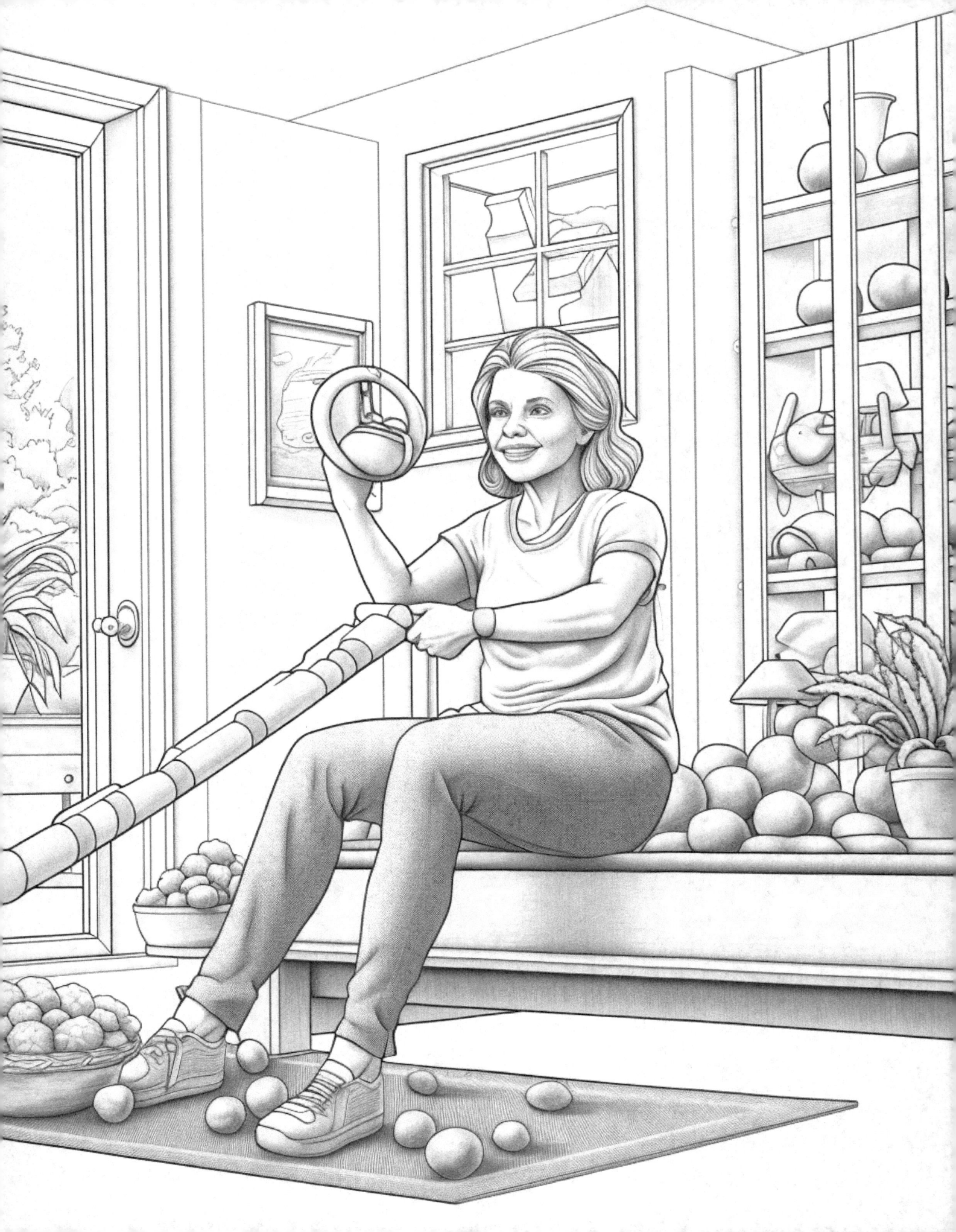

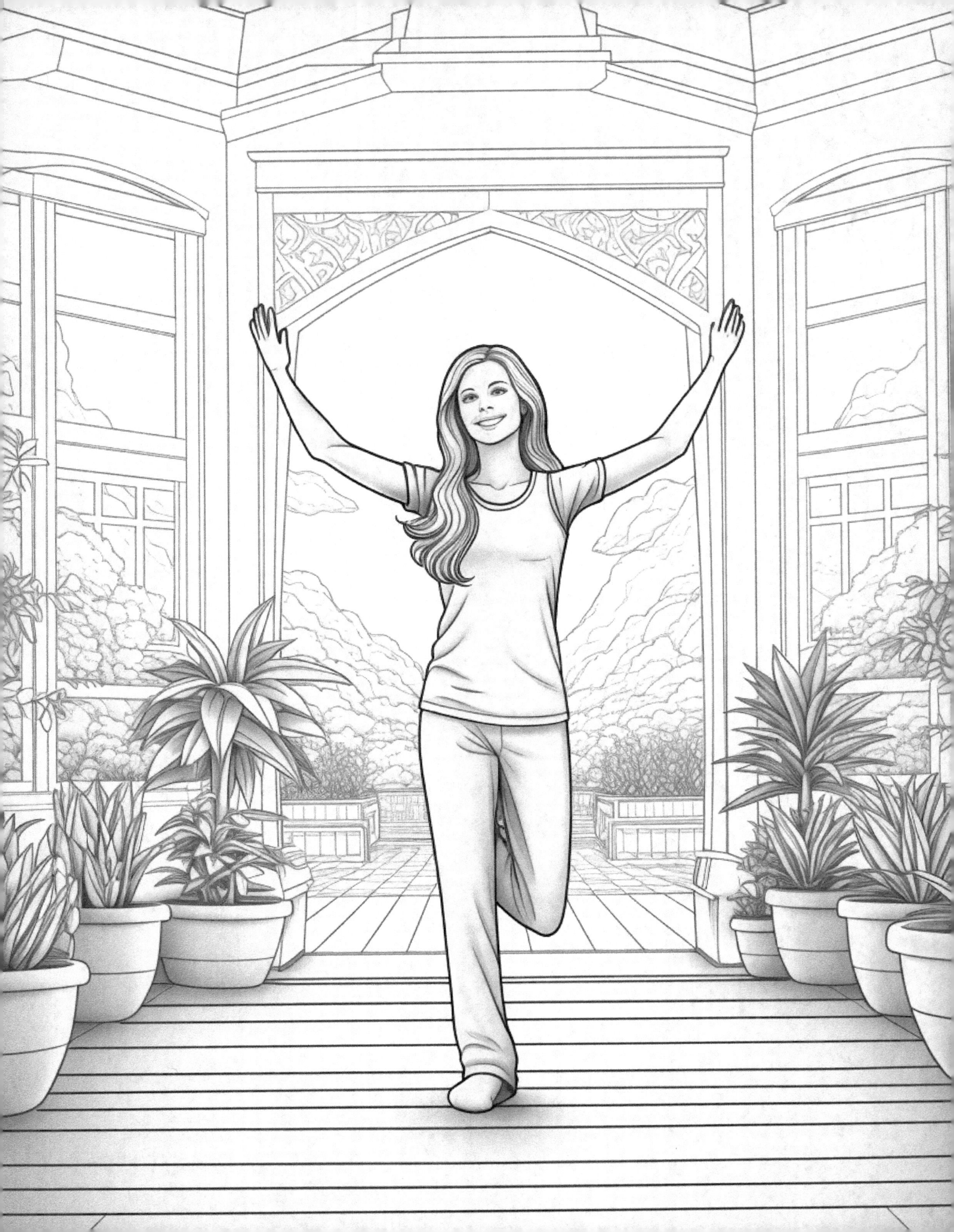

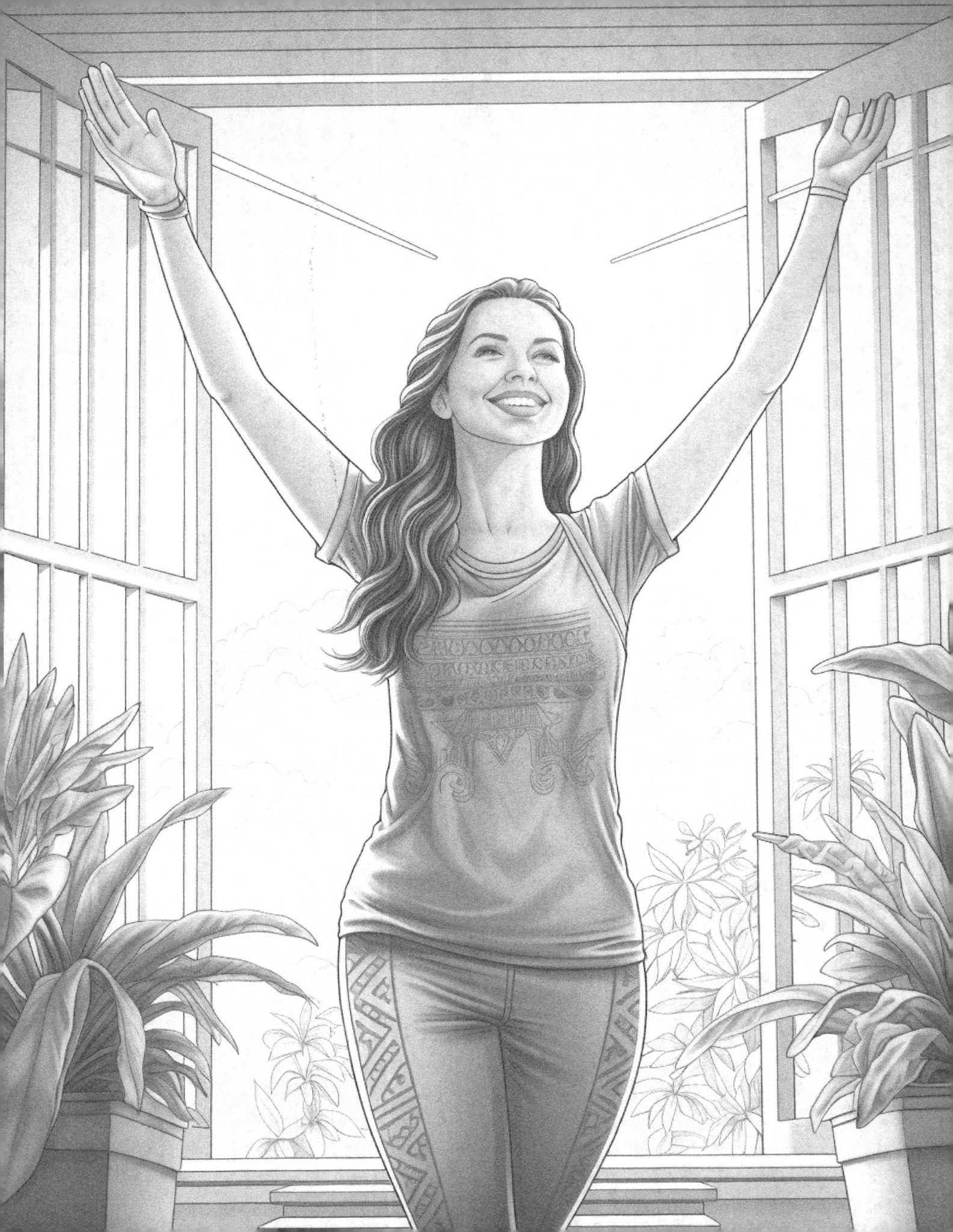

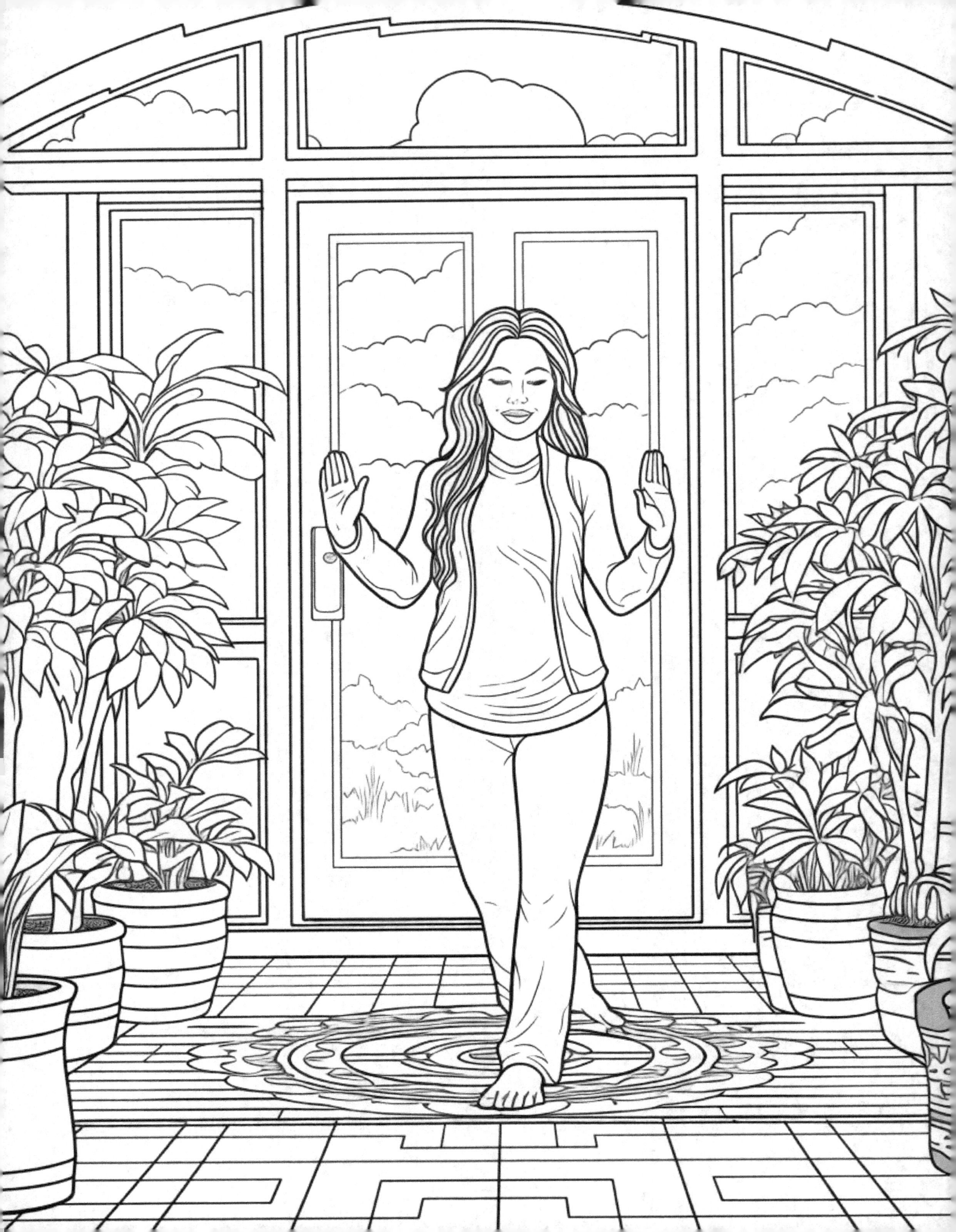

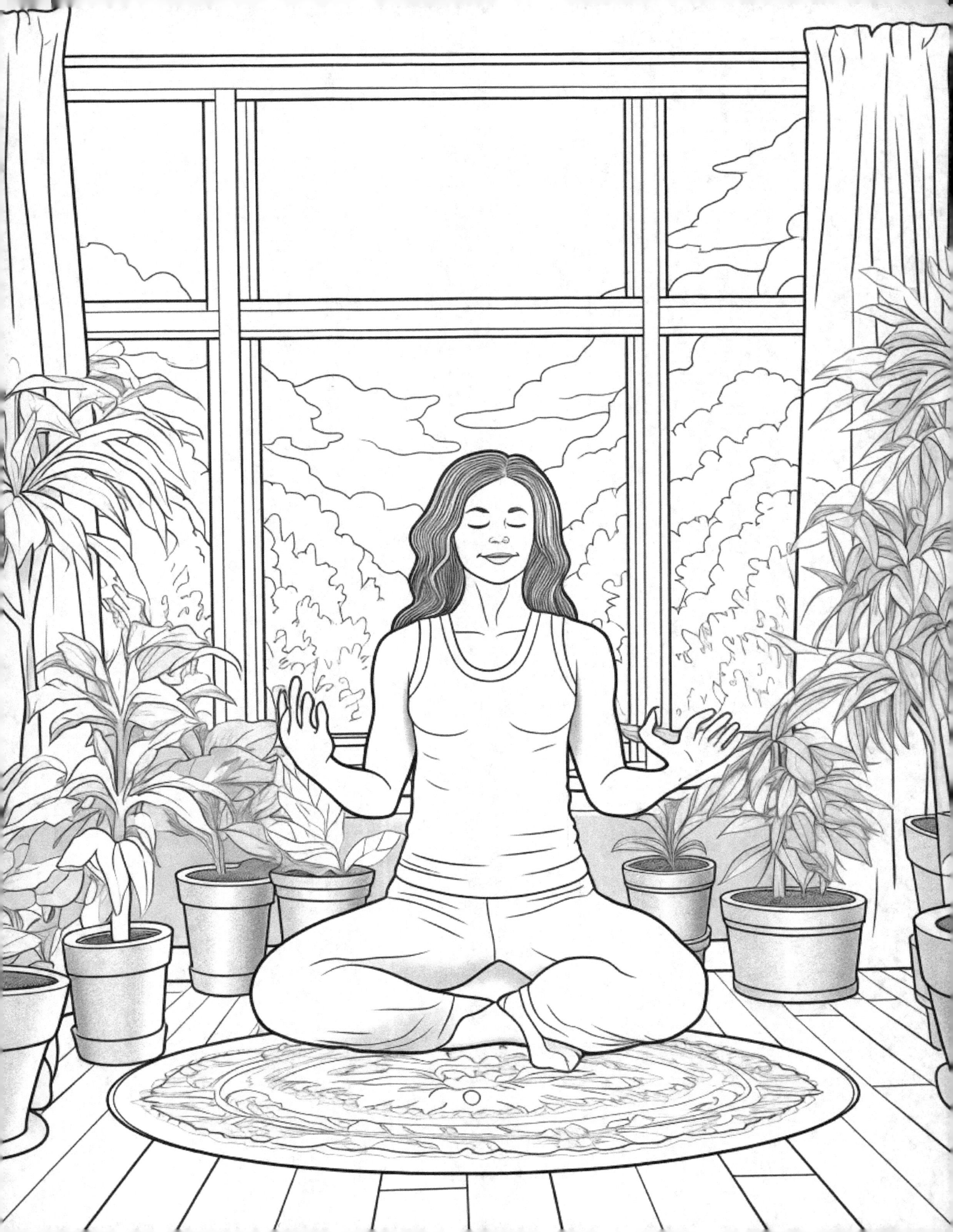

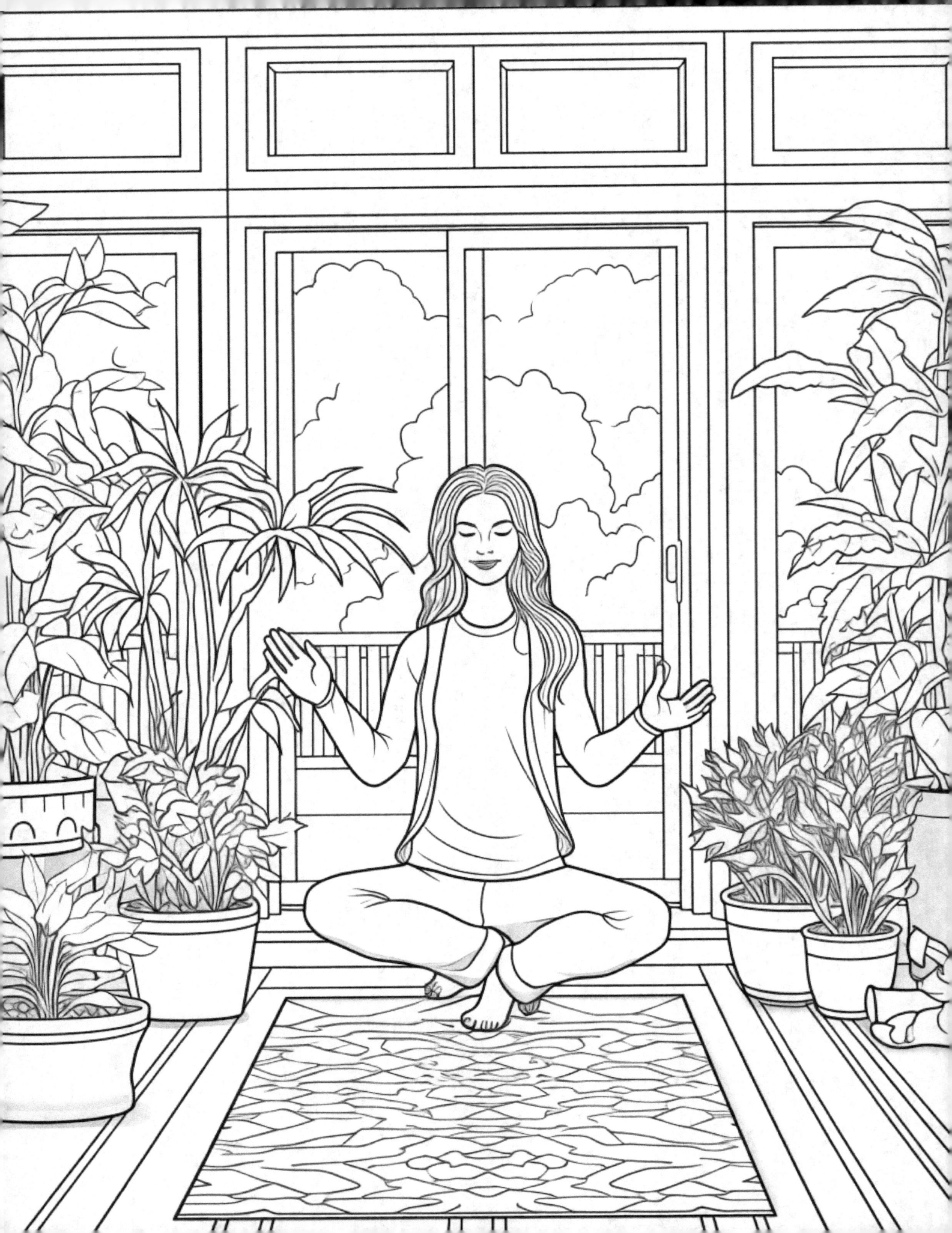

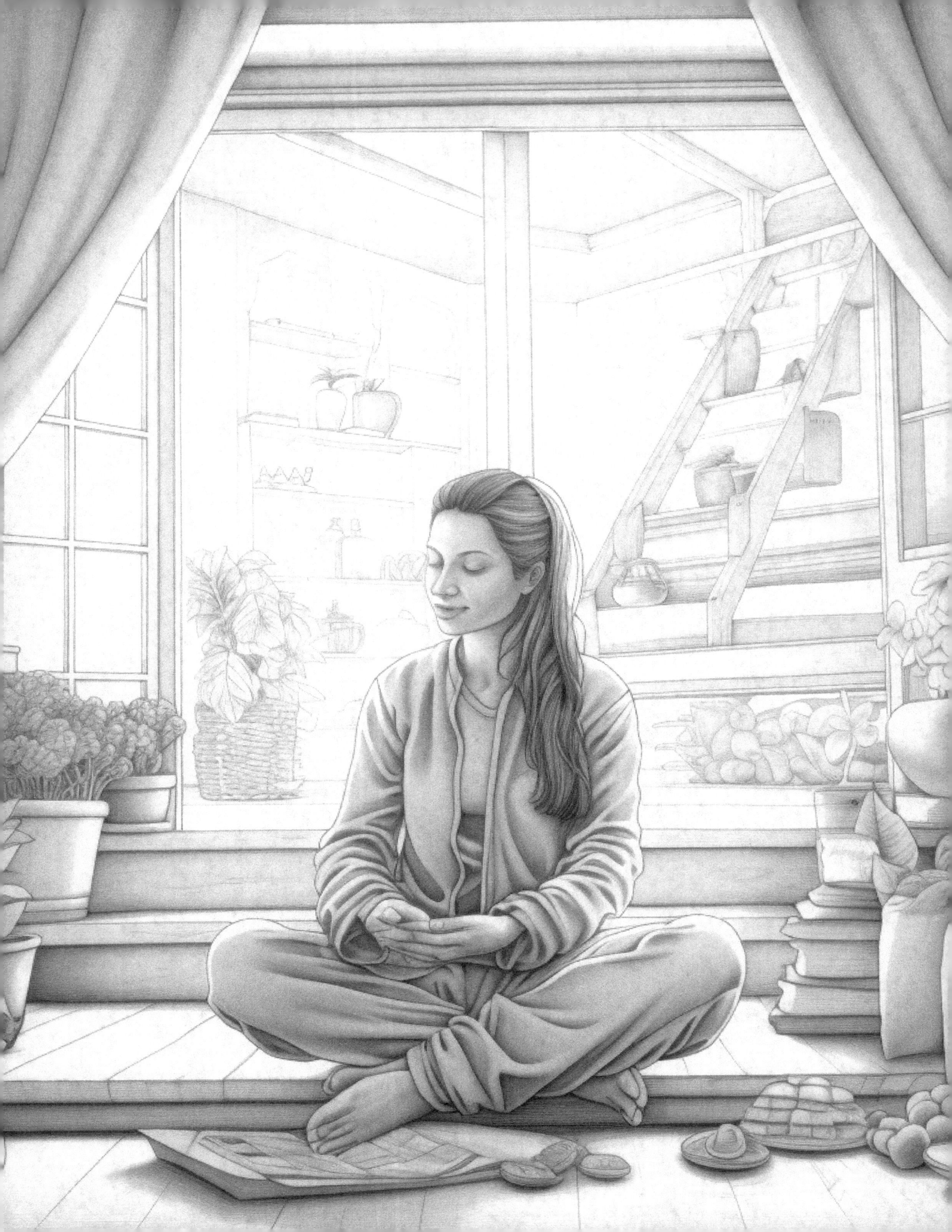

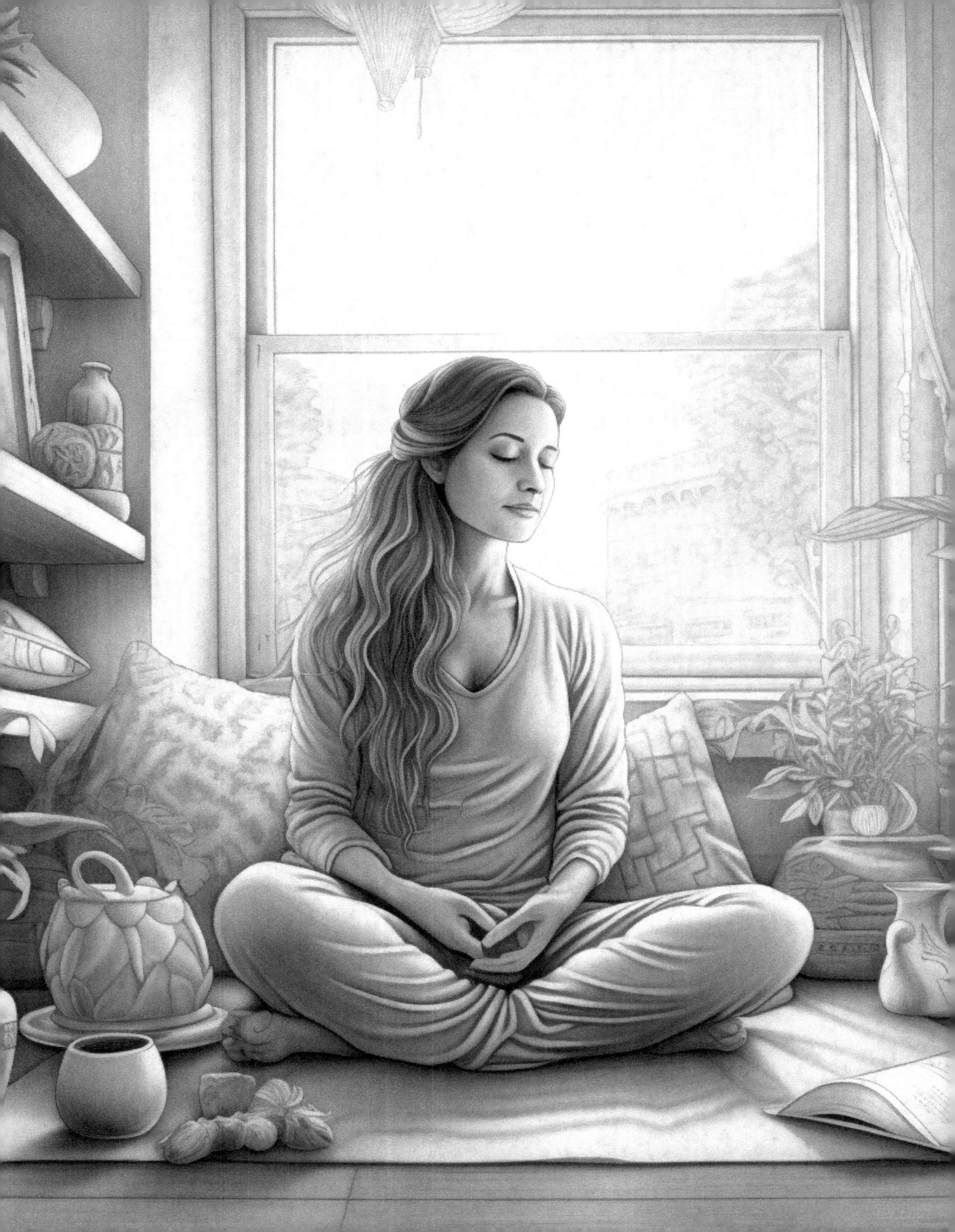

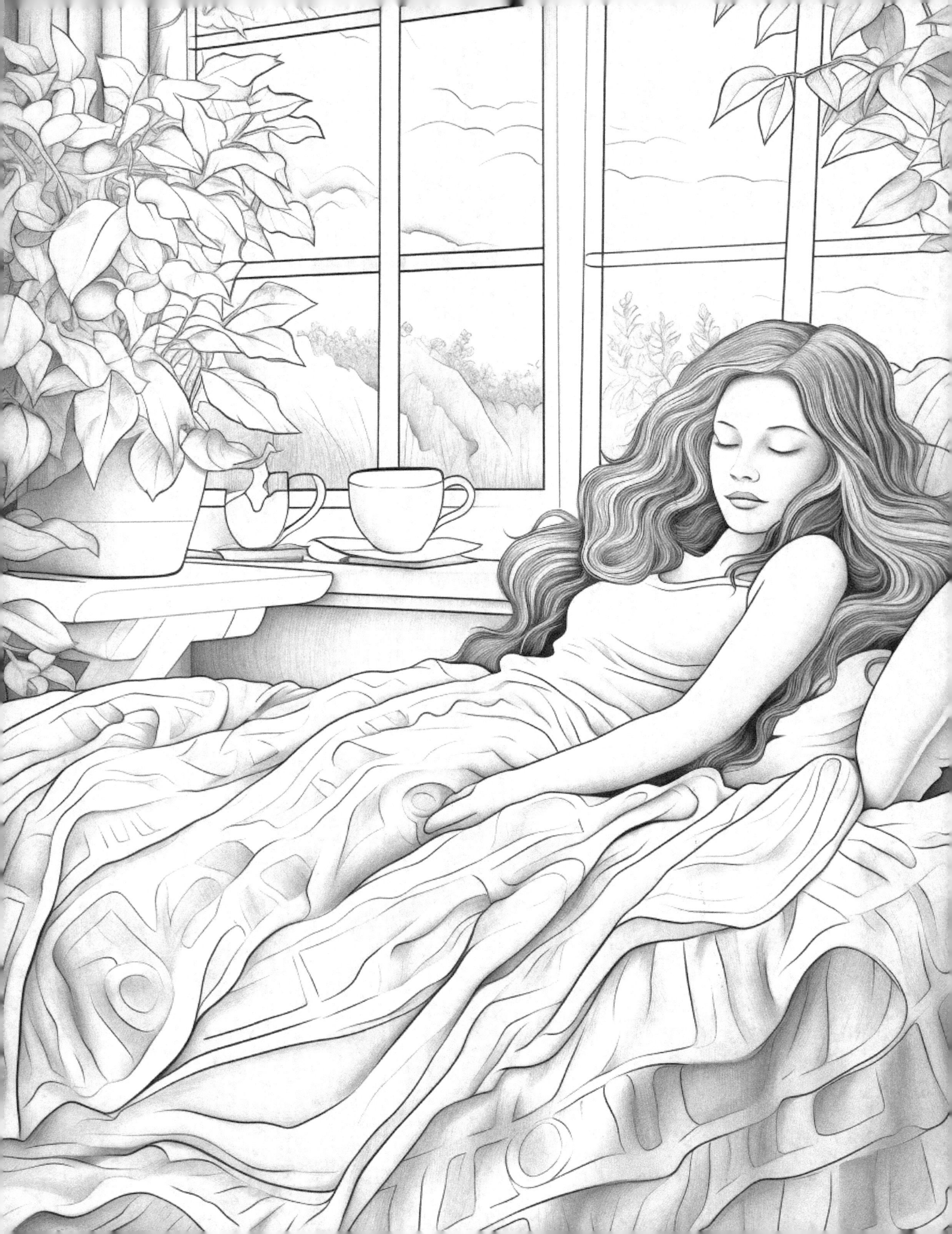

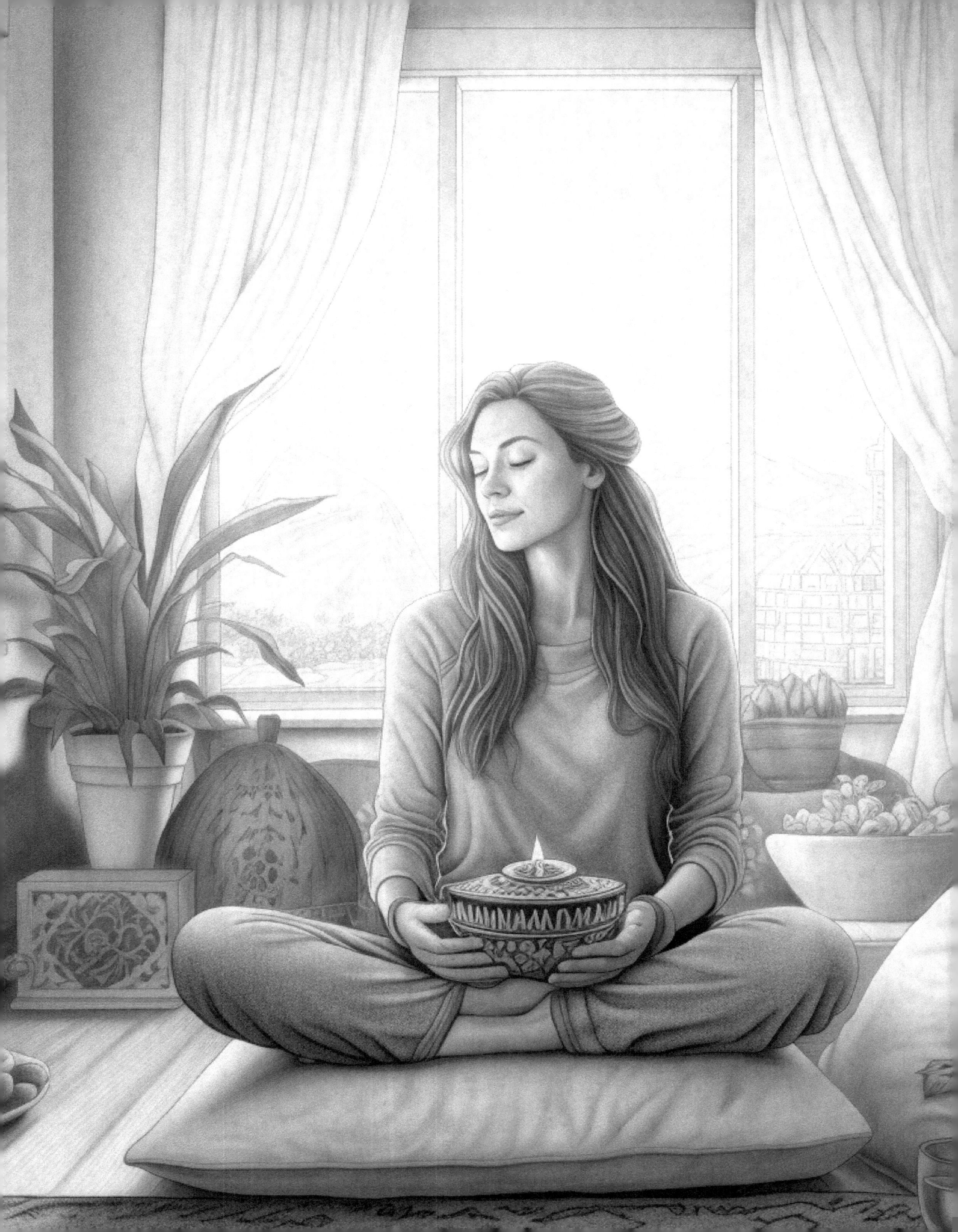

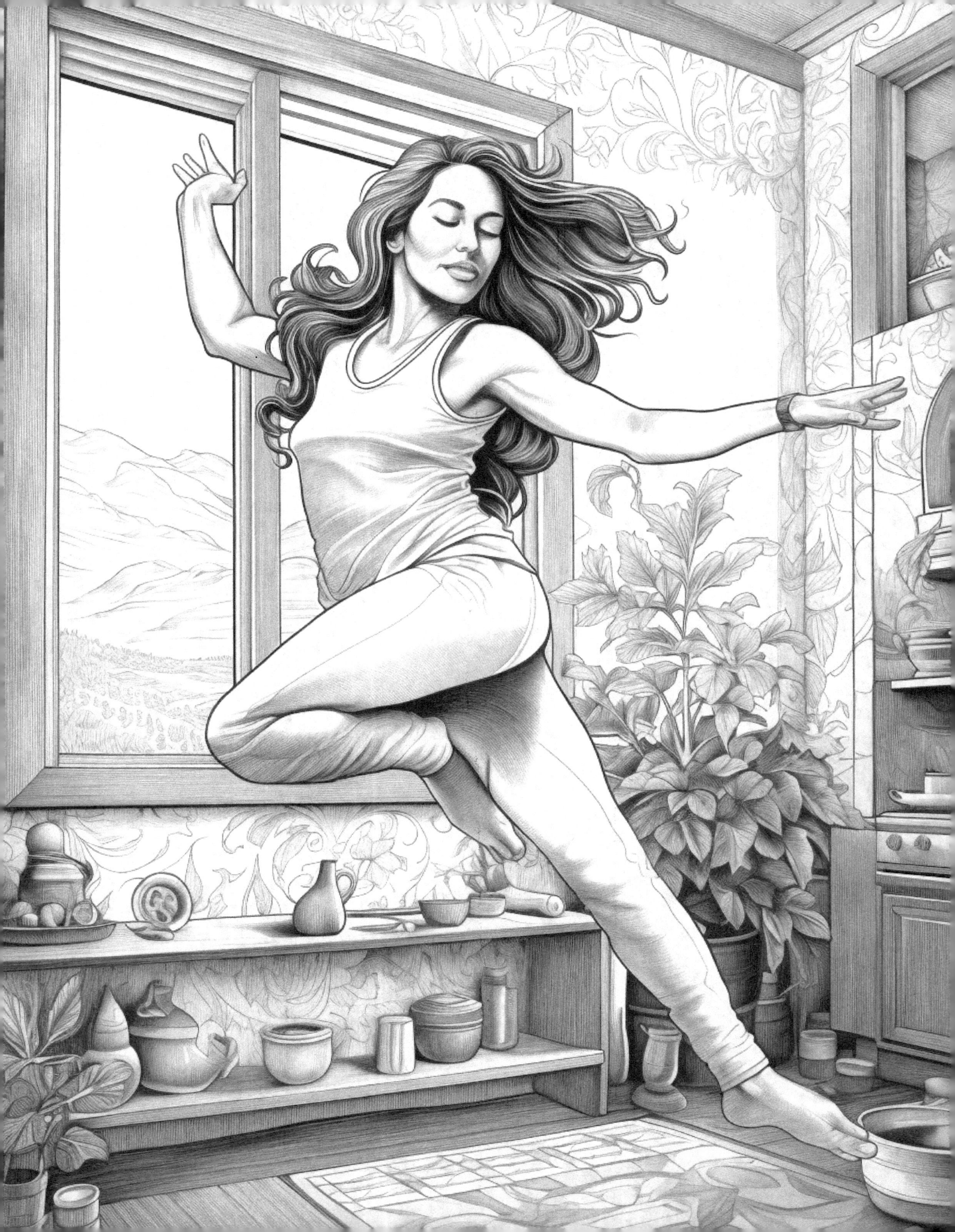

THE END

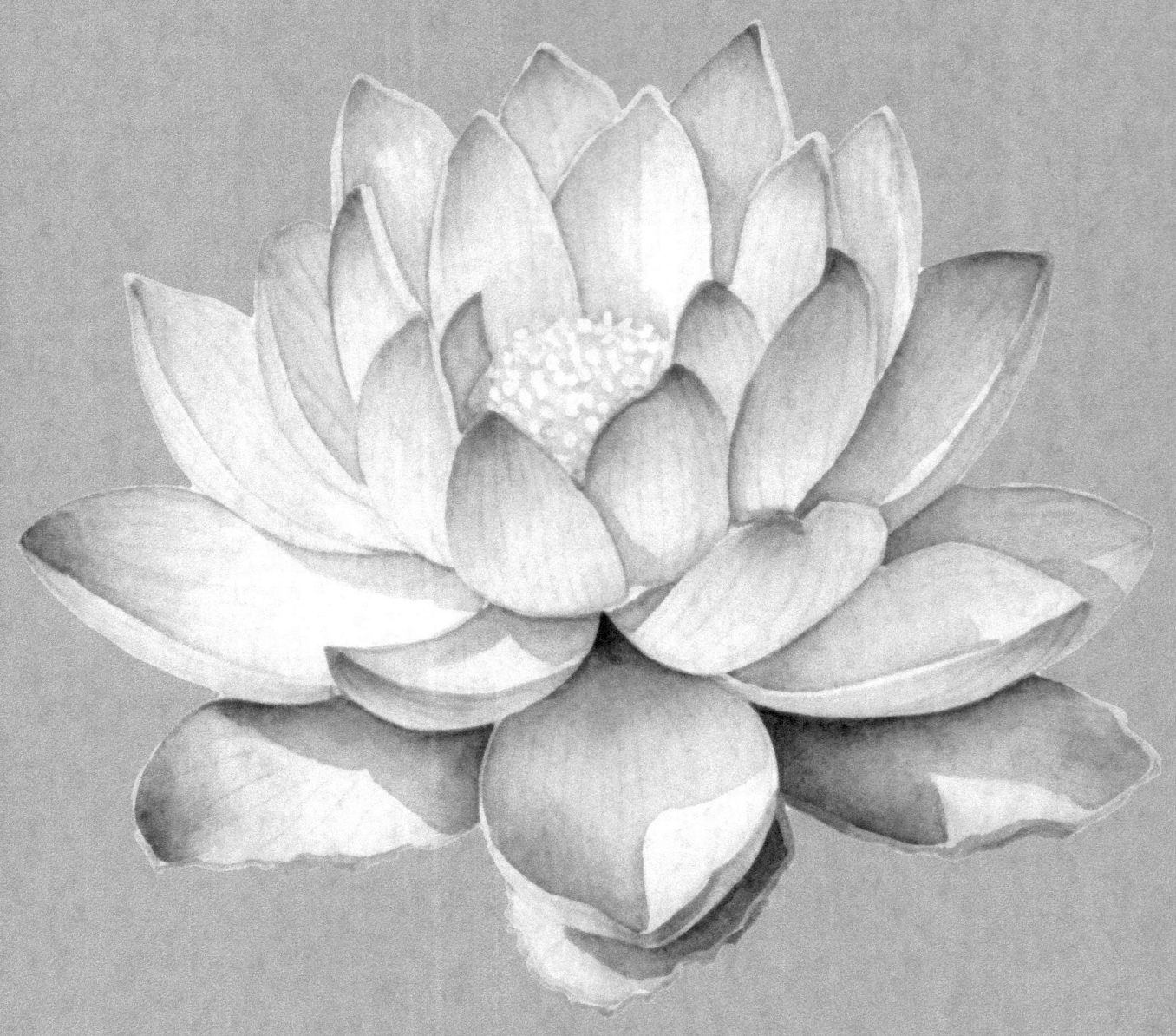